CRAFTS

OF THE MIDDLE AGES™

THE CRAFTS AND CULTURE OF A
MEDIEVAL CASTLE

Joann Jovinelly and Jason Netelkos

rosen
central™

The Rosen Publishing Group, Inc., New York

For Mom, a spirited and creative woman who taught me it was possible to make magic

Published in 2007 by The Rosen Publishing Group, Inc.
29 East 21st Street, New York, NY 10010

Library of Congress Cataloging-in-Publication Data

Jovinelly, Joann.
The crafts and culture of a Medieval castle/Joann Jovinelly and Jason Netelkos.—1st ed.
   p. cm.—(Crafts of the Middle Ages). Includes index.
ISBN 1-4042-0760-0 (library binding)
1. Handicraft—Europe—History—To 1500—Juvenile literature. 2. Castles—Europe—History—Juvenile literature. 3. Middle Ages Europe—History—Juvenile literature.
I. Netelkos, Jason. II. Title. III. Series: Jovinelly, Joann. Crafts and culture of the Middle Ages.
TT55.J672 2007
355.109'02—dc22

2005032974

Manufactured in the United States of America

Note to Parents
Some of these projects require tools or materials that can be dangerous if used improperly. Adult supervision will be necessary when projects require the use of a craft knife, cut aluminum, plaster of paris, or pins and needles. Before starting any of the projects in this book, you may want to cover your work area with newspaper or plastic. In addition, we recommend using a piece of thick cardboard to protect surfaces while cutting with craft or mat knives. We encourage you to discuss safety with your children and note in advance which projects may require your supervision.

CONTENTS

Castles often conjure romantic images about the ways in which Europeans lived during the Middle Ages, the period between the fall of the Roman Empire in 476 and the fifteenth century. On the contrary, castles played a practical role in protecting noble families and townspeople from attackers. The word "castle" comes from the Latin word *castellum*, which means "fortress."

During the decline of the Roman Empire, western Europe fell victim to hosts of invasions (and migrations) from various Asiatic, Germanic, and Slavic peoples of the rest of Europe and the East, collectively referred to as "barbarians" by the Romans. Fear and turmoil were widespread. It was nearly impossible for Rome to continually defend its borders, which had once reached as far as the

This Book of Hours, or collection of personalized texts of devotion for liturgical hours, belonged to Jean de Berry, a noble of fifteenth-century France. Illustrated here is the September grape harvest at the duke's Chateau de Saumur.

present-day countries of England, France, and Germany. By the fifth century, the empire had completely collapsed when Rome itself was sacked. Contributing to the final blow was a combination of infighting, political corruption, and economic strife. The Roman way of life had ended, giving way to chaos. Some historians still refer to this time as the Dark Ages, since advancements in literacy and culture ended.

The old Roman political system would eventually give way to dozens of fragmented kingdoms, each competing for land, wealth, and power. These kingdoms were partially made up of the various Germanic groups—Goths, Franks, Lombards, Vandals, Angles, and Saxons—that had invaded the empire as its power and ability to defend itself

The nations that eventually emerged out of western Europe are pictured on this map, which was taken from a sixteenth-century atlas by Abraham Ortelius called Theatre of the World. *It is considered the world's first modern atlas.*

weakened. Later, in the eighth century, the Norsemen, or Vikings, began to take advantage of this lack of centralized authority, especially in northern Europe. They traveled along European waterways, pillaging towns along their routes. Their raids proved to be especially disruptive. To help ward off invaders, Europeans built castles, first out of wood and later out of stone. Castles were erected in well-chosen areas, such as on mountainsides and next to waterways where they were partially protected from invasion. They were also built at strategic points such as along trading routes.

Out of necessity, castle building dominated the Middle Ages. In many cases, entire towns developed around castles because peasants found both work and safety within their walls. It is for these reasons that castles were important to all classes of society, from the nobles who lived in them to the peasants, workers, and knights who helped maintain and defend them. The castle design worked so well as a defensive structure, in fact, that thousands were built throughout western Europe during this period.

EARLY CASTLES

The first European castles were erected in France during the ninth century, after the death of Charlemagne. As the

Carolingian Empire, which had stretched over present-day France, Germany, and northern Italy, collapsed, leaders began to fight with one another. This led to the need for defensive structures. The castle's unique protective design quickly spread throughout western Europe. (The idea of a fortified castle was not original to Europeans, however. The Japanese had built castles since the fourth century. Europeans also gleaned many design ideas from the Islamic and Byzantine castles they encountered while trying to recapture the Holy Lands from Muslims during the religious wars known as the Crusades, 1096–1291.)

In the eleventh century, castles were especially important to the Norman conquest of England by William, Duke of Normandy (William the Conqueror). After winning England in the Battle of Hastings in 1066, he set down to survey his territory. William, who ruled until 1087, needed to defend his land, subdue millions of Saxons, and support his small army. His only choice was to order his men to build a network of castles, each one of them a stronghold of defense at a strategic point. Because of the speed at which the castles were needed, he chose the simple motte-and-bailey style. These were made entirely of wood.

A typical castle from this period was built upon a mound of earth called a motte. (A few had large raised enclosures called ringworks.) The motte was normally a mound between 15 and 30 feet (4 and 9 meters) high with a flat, circular top. Thorn bushes covered its sloping sides, which must have been difficult to scale to begin with. Around it, peasants were ordered to dig a huge ditch, to further help deter invaders. Sometimes streams and rivers helped "feed" these ditches, creating a moving waterway moat. Tall logs encircled the space on top of the motte, each of them fixed together as tightly as possible to create a palisade, or fence. Beyond the palisade was the castle keep, an inner stronghold or tower that was perched high on top of the motte. (During medieval times, keeps were called great towers or donjons.) Surrounding the keep was a circular walkway where the lord's soldiers would stand watch. While the castle's lord and his family lived high above the palisade in the keep, servants resided in smaller structures within the bailey below. The bailey was a detached, enclosed area accessible to the keep by a walkway and gate. It was also surrounded by a fence and a ditch. The bailey usually contained a main hall, enclosures for livestock, a forge (for metalworking), an armory, and a chapel. During times of conflict, townspeople rushed to the castle for protection.

Many variations of these motte-and-bailey castles were built in the century after the Norman conquest. Motte-and-bailey castles can be seen in the *Bayeux Tapestry*. This embroidery was commissioned in the 1070s by Bishop Odo of Bayeux, the half brother of William the Conqueror. It tells the story of the Norman conquest of England. Today, none of these wooden structures remain. Many were rebuilt on the same sites in stone, and where others once stood, only earthen mounds are left. At the time of William the Conqueror's death in 1087, there were eighty-six Norman castles in England.

FROM WOOD TO STONE

Before the eleventh century, the only monuments commonly built in stone were houses of worship. The earliest known stone tower keep was built in France, circa 950. Beginning at the end of the tenth century, wooden palisades were replaced by impressive stone walls called curtains, with sturdy wooden gates and watchtowers.

The first Norman castles made of stone took on a rectangular shape. One example of a typical Norman stone castle is the White Tower in the Tower of London. Today, this central keep has four turrets, three of them square and one circular. The circular turret housed England's first royal observatory. Over the centuries, the Tower of London has been used as a fortress and a prison. As a prison, it housed Queen Elizabeth I, two of Henry VIII's wives, and the famed explorer Sir Walter Raleigh.

Another stone castle built by the Normans can be seen in Essex, England. Colchester Castle in Colchester, the original Roman capital of England, was built largely from the remains of a Roman temple. Today, Colchester Castle houses a museum.

This Norman castle was built on the remains of a Roman fort. After the Norman conquest of England, William the Conqueror's half brother, Robert of Mortain, was granted Pevensey Castle.

Another typical example of a Norman stone castle is Dover Castle. It is situated on the coast of Kent, England, just twenty miles (thirty-two kilometers) from France. In the 1180s, William the Conqueror's grandson, Henry II, transformed what was once a Saxon fortress. The structure had been built from the remains of a Roman lighthouse into one of England's strongest castles. Henry II ordered his architect, Maurice the Engineer, to construct an elaborate keep out of stone that housed two chapels, three apartments for nobility, accommodations for the garrison, and large storage rooms. Two concentric outer walls were also added, each with projecting towers to aid in defense.

Windsor Castle was also begun during the reign of William the Conqueror in the 1070s and added to over the centuries since his death. Under the Normans, Windsor Castle was a motte and two baileys. Overlooking the river Thames, Windsor Castle, along with the Tower of London, is part of a ring of castles that surround the city.

DEFENDING THE CASTLE

Invaders found penetrating a castle's high stone walls exceedingly difficult since the walls had only a few slender windows. Still, they found logical ways to undermine even the most secure structures. Some castle walls were weakened by the constant chipping away of their stone, and other invaders would dig holes to try and enter the castle from underground or undermine its foundation.

One of the most effective ways in which to challenge a king was to surround the castle and remain there until its inhabitants starved to death, since supplies could not reach them during a siege. It is for this reason that most castles had a means for collecting rain on their roofs for such emergencies. If a king or lord thought his castle was about to be besieged, the butler was ordered to stock up on provisions. Indeed, the butler's task was often a difficult one. According to historical records, when it was believed that England's Salisbury Castle was about to be attacked in 1173, its butler gathered beans, wheat (for baking bread), bacon, cheese, salt, and malt (for brewing beer). Women and children were often referred to as "useless mouths" during times of attack. This was because they ate provisions without contributing to the defense of the castle.

Usually, kings and their lords planned in advance the steps to take in the event of an attack. They often tried to get out of town if they knew a siege might occur. Some would immediately surrender. Castle sieges were often

England's Windsor Castle, home to its royal family, dates back to the 1070s, when it was designed in wood under the direction of William the Conqueror. It has been constantly occupied and improved upon over the last 1,000 years and is now completely made of stone.

avoidable. In many cases, arrangements were made between the knights of the garrison and the attackers. This usually meant that a castle could be under attack for a defined period—usually thirty days. If outside relief did not arrive within that time, the castle and its residents surrendered. This process was eventually referred to as the honors of war. In this type of surrender, the victors would treat the surrendering residents honorably by not sacking the place and even allowing residents to keep some of their possessions.

If invaders did gain access to the castle, their efforts were a struggle. Before having any chance to get behind castle walls, they had to cross a water-filled moat (sometimes just a grassy ditch), sometimes with a current that could possibly sweep a person under. Entrance to the gatehouse was also nearly impossible. An iron portcullis, a grilled metal sliding door that could be lowered from the gatehouse walls, protected the wooden door. Sometimes a second portcullis was lowered at the end of the gatehouse, which was like a long two-story hall in a separate structure outside of the castle. If an intruder made it past the first entrance, defenders often showered him from above with scalding hot water or oil through small openings called machicolations. This would give defenders enough time to wound their attackers and close the second portcullis.

Some castles also contained a barbican, a fortified gateway in front of a castle entrance that allowed defenders to trap their attackers. Few intruders even got as far as to experience these fates, since most were shot by arrows or hit with stones outside the castle grounds. Knights of the garrison hid behind crenellations, raised "shields" (merlons) on the tops of towers, and shot their arrows through the "gaps" (crenels) from a position of safety. Knights also peered out of specially designed castle windows for safety. These openings were extremely narrow on the outside, which prevented attackers from hitting them with stones or arrows but allowed the knights to see and take aim at their intruders. During the thirteenth century,

when castles were built with circular towers, the stairs were always twisted to the right since it prevented right-handed attackers from swinging their swords while climbing up. These advancements in defense were made over time and, like castles themselves, were continually improved upon. Among the last of these advancements was the development of concentric castles, or castles with rings of defensive walls. In this thirteenth-century design, the inner walls were usually taller than the outer walls. This allowed defenders to shoot over the heads of their peers maintaining the outer defenses. One example of a concentric castle is Beaumaris Castle on the Isle of Anglesey in Wales.

BEHIND CASTLE WALLS

During the Middle Ages, the constant dividing of land contributed to the development of feudalism, a political and social system that prevailed throughout western Europe. The lords who were granted land by the king were also given the right to protect that land with fortified buildings. Lords then offered land grants to vassals in exchange for their allegiance and help in protecting the castle.

Some castles were small and had few servants. Others were much larger and housed and employed hundreds of people. Despite their differences in size, all castles had common elements, such as the great hall, the main room of the castle, a kitchen (sometimes a separate building since fire was a risk), and apartments for the lord and his family.

The castle staff included the garrison, foot soldiers, and archers that could be called to duty at any time. All of their armor and other equipment—longbows, crossbows, and arrows—had to be maintained. Horses and livestock were also kept on the castle grounds, requiring grooms, stable hands, and even blacksmiths to replace horseshoes. A steward organized all of the lord's servants, while reeves and bailiffs collected rents from vassals and managed the lord's farms. In addition, the lord and lady had a staff of personal servants.

CASTLES IN DECLINE

As local warfare ceased in the fifteenth century, the need for castles faded. Societies became increasingly stable. More people wanted to live in comfortable, private homes and not the dark, cold stone fortifications of the past. Many castles found other uses as military bases, while the rest fell into disrepair or were sold for the value of their stones. The importation of gunpowder from Asia and the inventions of cannons and artillery in western Europe in the fourteenth century also contributed to the decline of castle building.

Today, castles give us a fascinating glimpse into what life was like during the medieval period. Although many are now in ruin, they will forever be a magical symbol of the Middle Ages.

Life in a Medieval Castle

Although the wealthy nobles who lived in a castle experienced every advantage the medieval period could offer, privacy was rarely among those luxuries. All living quarters in a castle were shared among family members, except for the lord himself, who had a private chamber. The lord and his family lived in the castle keep, where the strongest and safest rooms were housed. If a town was attacked, all of the townspeople would rush to the castle for safe hiding in the keep.

The great hall was where a lord received his guests, conducted business, and ate his meals. The great hall was also where the lord, his family, and his guests were entertained in the evening during meals. These were often elaborate, multicourse affairs that lasted hours. The interior of a castle was mostly dark since the windows were narrow. It was also damp, cold, and smoky since the hearth fires were the only source of heat. Although they were sparsely furnished and lit only by candlelight or oil lamp, castle interiors were painted and had colorful carpets and tapestries hanging from their walls. Toward the end of the Middle Ages, cupboards called ambries were

Pictured in this photograph is the great hall in Switzerland's Chillon Castle, which dates from the twelfth century. During the Middle Ages, homes were sparsely furnished, even for nobles.

created for storage in castle walls. Chairs were few, but benches and chests doubled as beds and seats.

A typical day for a lord meant rising early to attend Mass in the castle chapel. After church services, he would eat a light meal of cheese and bread and then begin the business of the day: listening to complaints, collecting rents, making decisions, or hearing news of potential attackers nearing the castle. By midday, a large meal was prepared by his staff and delivered to him. After eating, he might go hunting on his grounds for deer, practice fencing, or ride around on horseback. By sunset, it was time to eat again, and this lighter meal was commonly accompanied by a variety of entertainers, including poets, musicians, acrobats, jugglers, or jesters. A chamberlain prepared his lord's chamber for a night's rest, which usually began early. Lifestyles for noble-women were somewhat similar, and they could act on behalf of their lords and make decisions for them in their absence.

A servant confides secrets to a noble woman in this miniature medieval painting from France. Although castle furnishings were few, colored tiles, woolen tapestries, and richly colored fabrics adorned cold, drafty rooms and protected people from rodents and insects while they slept.

England's Bodiam Castle, located in East Sussex, is a perfect example of a late medieval moated castle. Sir Edward Dalyngrigge, who received permission to build it by the king on the site where his manor once stood, erected it in 1385.

Model of a Castle

Create a copy of the fourteenth-century castle at Bodiam, England, with its round crenellated towers and narrow, arched windows.

YOU WILL NEED
- 2 large, round oat containers with lids
- 2 long, narrow cracker boxes
- 3 trash bag boxes
- 2 half-gallon milk cartons
- Masking tape
- Cardboard
- Glue
- Black marker/pencil
- Ruler
- Scissors
- Craft paint (gray or white; light and dark brown)
- Paintbrushes/sponges
- Bowl/glue-water mixture (for papier-mâché)
- Newspaper strips

Step 1
Take one of the trash bag boxes and cut a rounded door, as shown. Next, cut the tops off of your milk cartons and set them aside. Flip the oat containers upside down. Set them aside. Seal any openings of your boxes with masking tape.

Step 2
Next, assemble the boxes and containers. Start with the trash bag box with the cut doorway and tape one cracker box to each of its sides. Next, tape the other two trash bag boxes to the front of each cracker box. Tape one upside-down milk carton to each cracker box. (The milk cartons should be set back by several inches to achieve the look of Bodiam Castle.) Finally, attach an oat container to the front corner of each milk carton. Reinforce with masking tape.

Step 3
After you are satisfied with your arrangement, dampen strips of newspaper with your glue-water mixture and apply them with a paintbrush. Repeat this process until

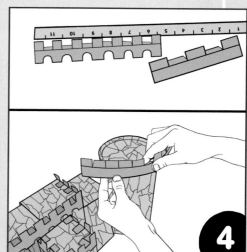

the structure is covered in glued paper strips. Allow time to dry between layers.

Step 4

Next, cut cardboard strips. These strips can be a variety of lengths, but they should all be 1½ inches in width. Position your strips horizontally. Measure and draw a horizontal line along each strip ½ inch from the top. To make the crenellations, draw vertical lines at either 1-inch or ½-inch points from this line. (One-inch crenellations are for the oat and milk cartons and ½-inch crenellations are for the cracker and trash bag boxes. Cut arches directly under each ½-inch crenellation, as shown.) Fold down alternate tabs and use those to attach the crenellated strips to the castle with glue.

Step 5

After the castle has dried, paint it gray or white. Next, cut a sponge into various shapes and set aside. Paint the castle again, this time using a brush and a light brown color.

Step 6

Add detail by dipping sponge pieces in shades of brown that are darker or lighter than your base color and randomly applying them to exterior walls. After the paint has dried, draw windows with a black marker.

The Great Hall

T he bigger and more important a king or lord was, the more impressive his castle's great hall. Parties that followed a town's ceremonies and feasts, such as weddings, christenings, saints' holidays, and Christmas took place in the great hall. Although these were community celebrations, only the influential were permitted inside. The rest of the townspeople remained outside, where they would be brought food. Entertainment was abundant during such occasions, and most great halls had an area for poets, musicians, minstrels, and acrobats to perform.

Walls of the great hall were usually lavishly decorated with tapestries, drapes, and carpets. Ceilings were high and usually made with timber. Floors were stone or wood. They were sometimes strewn with sweet-smelling herbs. Three or four hearths burned day and night. Upon entering the great hall,

The midday meal was the biggest event of the day to take place in the great hall. It was announced by trumpeters, and any visiting distinguished guests were expected to join the lord and his lady.

servants often washed important guests' hands and faces using water provided in basins situated at the door openings.

If it was mealtime, everyone had a pre-assigned seat according to his or her social status. Members of the lower classes sat away from the main table. The lord and his guests often had seating that was raised above the rest to show their stature. Night meals often lasted for hours, and afterward, tables were moved

A group of peasants enjoy a meal of pottage and bread in the countryside. While nobles ate lavish meals inside, excess food and scraps were often given to peasants living nearby.

so straw mattresses called palliasses could be brought in for sleeping.

At night, when hearth fires were dimmed, tapestries kept the room warm. Large tapestries like those from the fifteenth-century series The Hunt of the Unicorn date back to medieval times. First a symbol of Christ, the unicorn evolved into a symbol of love and marriage. These tapestries, which hang in the Cloisters, a part of New York's Metropolitan Museum of Art, were originally made in the fifteenth century in northern Europe, most likely on the occasion of an aristocratic woman's marriage. (The pomegranates in the tree are symbols of marriage and fertility.) Later, they hung in a castle in France belonging to the Rochefoucauld family. John D. Rockefeller purchased the tapestries for the Metropolitan Museum in the 1920s.

The Unicorn in Captivity *is part of the collection of New York City's Metropolitan Museum of Art. Symbols in this tapestry reveal details about its original owner.*

Unicorn Tapestry*

Create a miniature copy of a unicorn in captivity, a detail from the Franco-Flemish fifteenth-century tapestry series The Hunt of the Unicorn.

* ADULT SUPERVISION IS ADVISED FOR THIS CRAFT.

YOU WILL NEED

- Burlap
- Paper
- Felt
- Colored markers
- Felt-tip pen
- White fabric marker
- Paintbrush
- Pencil
- Yarn
- Sewing needle
- Straight pins
- String
- Scissors

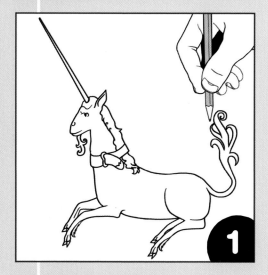

Step 1
Draw a picture of a unicorn on your paper about the size you want it to appear on your tapestry. (You can photocopy and enlarge the illustration shown here.) Cut it out with scissors and pin it to the center of your burlap.

Step 2
Lay your burlap on a protected work surface. Trace along the edge of the unicorn with a felt-tip pen. Remove the paper and draw details such as the unicorn's eyes, mane, and collar. Draw a fence around the unicorn by making a series of ovals and straight lines. Draw a tree trunk, as shown. Color the fence with a light brown or orange marker.

Step 3
Draw and color leaves for your tree, as shown. Surround the entire fence and tree with flowers. Use a green marker to make curved lines for flower stems and other markers to make petals.

Step 4

After all of your flowers are colored, use a white fabric marker to color the unicorn. Color all of the burlap surrounding the flowers, unicorn, fence, and tree with a dark green marker.

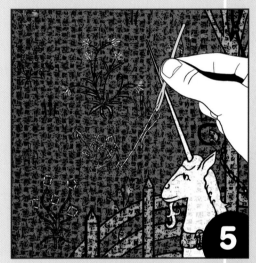

Step 5

After the coloring is complete, you can embroider the tapestry. Use your drawing as you would an embroidery pattern. Thread your sewing needle with yarn or floss and tie a knot at one end. Thread it through the back of the burlap to begin random embroidering.

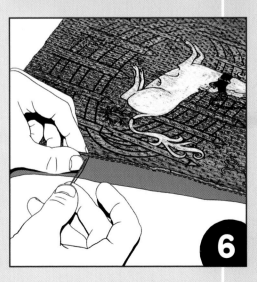

Step 6

Fold a ½-inch border around the edge of the burlap and pin it in place. Cut a piece of string, approximately 25 inches, and knot it at each end. Cut a piece of felt to fit the reverse side of the burlap. Sew the edges onto the felt, removing pins as you complete each side. To hang your tapestry, sew the knotted ends of the string between the felt and burlap at each top corner.

The Garrison

T he group of knights whose job it was to protect the castle and the lord's family was called a garrison. The knights of the garrison lived in their own dwellings and were stationed at the castle for a set period. During times of siege, knights performed the crucial duties of protecting the castle. Each knight had his own coat of chain mail, a steel helmet, and a wooden or metal shield that was often decorated to reflect his family lineage. A knight was responsible for paying for and maintaining his own equipment. Knights often became landowners since the king or lord paid them in parcels of land in exchange for their protection. By the late Middle Ages, when there were many more knights and fewer parcels of land to be given, knights were hired to live at the castle permanently.

Increasingly, only men of nobility became knights. Becoming a knight required years of training, which began around the age of seven, when a young boy served his father or was sent to another household to learn how to be a

The French knight in this fifteenth-century manuscript illumination is wearing a basinet. This was a common helmet used for jousting during the Middle Ages because it protected the face while still allowing partial vision.

page. While learning how to ride a horse, a page also learned academic skills, such as reading and writing. Pages were usually taught eloquent manners, how to dance and sing, and how to fight with a sword. By the time they were about fourteen years old, they went on to become squires (apprentices to knights). As a knight's squire, a teenage boy cleaned and maintained his knight's armor, took care of his horses, and

learned to fight. A squire was expected to go into battle alongside his knight. Because training was so difficult, not all squires became knights. And some even died in battle before they were knighted. If a squire made it to age twenty-one and his training was completed, he would be knighted in a formal ceremony and "sir" would be attached to his name.

By the year 1200, the church had taken over these ceremonies. Becoming a knight was nearly considered a religious sacrament. To prepare, a candidate for knighthood took a bath in rosewater the night before the ceremony (bathing was infrequent during the Middle Ages). Afterward, he put on a clean white tunic and a red robe, and knelt before an alter for ten hours in front of his armor to more fully understand the importance of his passage into knighthood. On the morning of the ceremony, a mass was held at dawn and a knight would take his vows. Once he was presented with his spurs and armor, which were blessed, an older knight tapped his shoulders with a sword and the ceremony was complete. A large celebration, games, and mock duels followed the ceremony.

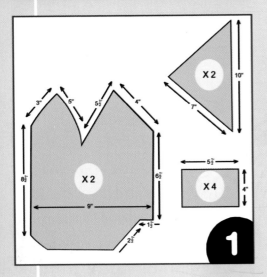

Knight's Helmet*

If you were a knight about to take part in the Hundred Years' War (1337–1453) between France and England, you would have worn a helmet like this one.
* Please ask a parent to assist you, or wear protective gloves while handling cut metal.

YOU WILL NEED

- 2 large, disposable aluminum baking pans
- Scissors
- Awl
- Hole puncher
- Paper fasteners
- Paper
- Pencil
- Marker
- Ruler
- Protective gloves
- Construction paper

Step 1

Use a pencil and ruler to draw the pattern pictured in Step 1 on paper and cut it out, being sure to recreate its exact dimensions. Remove the sides of both baking pans by cutting them along their bottom parameters. Next, use the paper pattern to trace the design onto both flat aluminum sheets in marker. Be mindful of the sharp edges! Carefully cut the patterns out of the two aluminum sheets. Set them aside and put on your protective gloves to handle the cut aluminum. Fold the sharp edges about ⅛ inch under along each edge, flattening them with the edge of a pencil as you fold.

Step 2

Take one of the two large shapes and flip it over so both pieces are facing each other, as shown. Overlap them by ½ inch and with an awl, make holes about 1 inch apart along the 6½-inch side, as shown. Join the pieces together with paper fasteners.

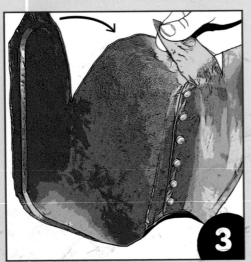

Step 3

Next, take the two 4-inch sides and overlap them in the same way. Make at least three holes along the seams with your awl and fasten them together using additional

paper fasteners to close the top of the helmet. Continue joining the other sides together as you did in Step 2.

Step 4
Take the two triangles and punch plenty of random holes in them. These will provide ventilation and will also help you to see out of the helmet. Next, fold both triangles in half. With an awl, make holes along the 7-inch seam of both triangles to join them together. Open the folds and fasten the two pieces together with paper fasteners.

Step 5
Cut a ½-inch slit in the top and bottom of the triangle fold. Make holes around the edge of the cone and fold the edge ½ inch outward. Position the helmet so the front is facing you. Make matching holes around the interior edges to fasten the cone to the helmet with more paper fasteners.

Step 6
Take the small rectangular pieces and make holes along the 5½-inch side to attach to the bottom of the cone and the bottom sides of the helmet as shown. Make a feather by cutting a 2-inch by 6-inch piece of construction paper.

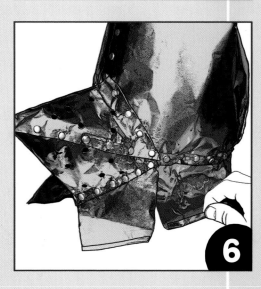

Knights in Tournament

When knights were not busy maintaining their armor or horses, and when enemies were not besieging the castles, they often practiced their fighting skills in tournaments. These were lavish mock battles that were sometimes difficult to discern from actual fighting. Instead of killing their opponents, knights captured them and held them for ransom. By the mid- to late twelfth century, these melees were gradually scaled down to just one event: the joust. Instead of full battles, the joust was a single engagement by two knights, either fought on foot or horseback. The church was against these tournaments, viewing them as unnecessary acts of violence. The church tried, rather unsuccessfully, to restrict tournaments by banning them on certain days and in certain seasons. Christian bishops forbid those knights who were killed a Christian burial if knights defied these restrictions.

Whether knights were a part of a medieval tournament or a single joust, the pageantry surrounding both events was carnival-like, complete with colorful

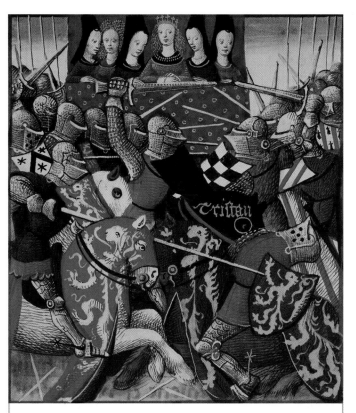

This fifteenth-century manuscript illustration shows knights in the midst of a tournament. War games such as this became an opportunity for a knight to keep up his skill in times of peace.

banners and decorations, plenty of food, and festivities that included dancing, storytelling, and reading fortunes. Rewards for knights who captured an opponent were handsome and included parcels of land, arms, or horses. Some tournaments were simulated battles. But throughout the Middle Ages, despite the enjoyment it brought to knights and nobles, tournaments succumbed to the criticism by the church as well as the expense to hold them. Eventually, all tournaments were reduced to brief military exercises or single jousts, complete with safety rules that were enforced at all times. Some sporting events that later became popular, such as throwing spears or javelins, were offshoots of these early medieval tournaments.

When hundreds of knights gathered together in a tournament or joust, among the only ways of distinguishing them on the field was by the symbols painted on their shields. These symbols eventually became known as coats of arms as they were also normally embroidered on a knight's sleeve. (Coats of arms also eventually came to be associated with family crests, and these symbols were combined and handed down from one generation to the next.)

The area on which these symbols, also known as charges, were painted on a shield was called its field. Common charges included crosses, bars, saltire (like an "x"), and pales (vertical stripes). As a knight aged and married or his wife had children, his coat of arms was often updated to reflect the changes in his family or to combine elements of his wife's family coat of arms with his own.

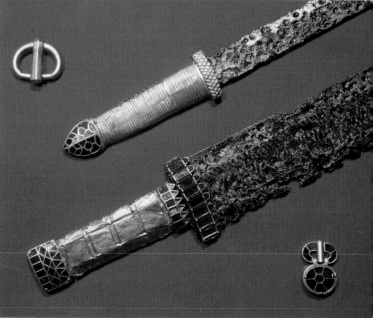

Top: A medieval manuscript touting the history of the kings of Aragon shows the coat of arms of Castile and Leon. Coats of arms were originally designed to help distinguish knights in battle.

Bottom: These fifth-century French swords feature detailed enameling on their handles. Some areas in France became known for their artisans who designed elaborate jewelry, belt buckles, and weaponry.

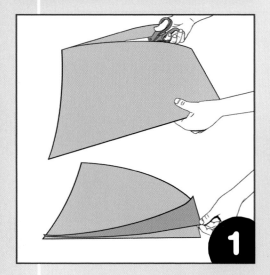

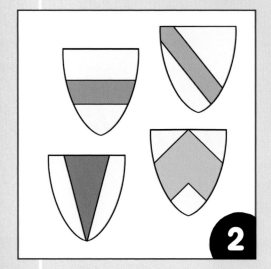

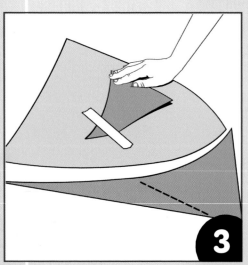

Sword and Shield

Imagine what your own coat of arms would look like if you were a knight. Paint your design using only the colors a knight would use. Make a sword to go with your shield and you'll be ready for a joust!

YOU WILL NEED

- Pizza box
- Craft/acrylic paint
- Paintbrush
- Masking tape
- Pencil
- Gesso or white primer
- Plaster of paris
- Paper towel roll
- Silver poster board
- Glue
- Craft knife/file
- Awl/clamp
- Wire hanger
- Scissors

Step 1

To make a shield, cut a pizza box in half and remove the sides. Draw an arc from the center of the bottom edge of one square to its top corner. Cut along this line. (Use the scrap piece as a template for the opposite side of the shield.) Next, cut along this second line making a shield shape. Set one of these pieces aside for Step 3.

Step 2

Cover the shield's edges with masking tape to give it a finished look. Paint it with a coat of white primer or gesso. Set aside to dry. Next, paint the entire shield in one color. This will be the field. Draw your coat of arms symbols, or charges, on the field. See the second illustration for sample period charges.

Step 3

Paint your shield's charges in black, red, blue, green, or purple. Metallic paint can be used as a field color or charge color, but not in both. After the paint has dried, cut a triangle from the piece you set aside in Step 1 and make a handle. Invert the triangle and attach it to the back of your shield with masking tape or glue.

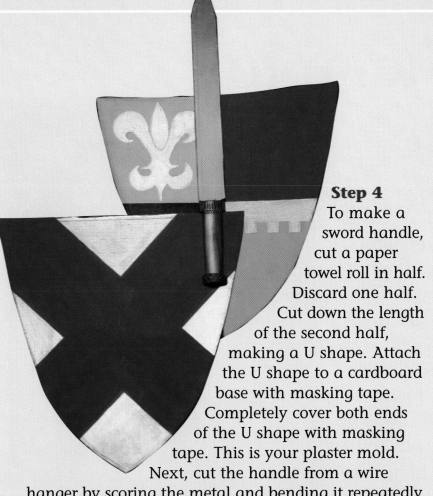

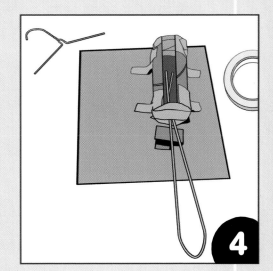

Step 4

To make a sword handle, cut a paper towel roll in half. Discard one half. Cut down the length of the second half, making a U shape. Attach the U shape to a cardboard base with masking tape. Completely cover both ends of the U shape with masking tape. This is your plaster mold. Next, cut the handle from a wire hanger by scoring the metal and bending it repeatedly. Fold the hanger in two equal lengths. Insert the hanger several inches in the mold by puncturing through the tape. Secure it in place with more tape.

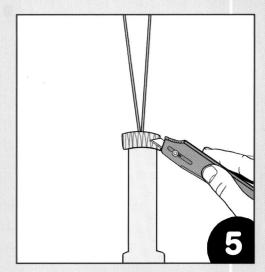

Step 5

Mix the plaster by following the package directions. Pour the plaster carefully into your U-shaped mold, filling it enough to cover all of the wire. Allow the mold to dry on a flat surface. Once dry, peel away the cardboard and tape. Use a craft knife and file to carve the plaster into the shape of a handle, as shown. You can use an awl to carve various designs.

Step 6

Brush away any dust and apply paint as you wish. To make a sword, cut two pieces of silver poster board in a sword shape and glue them together with the wire between them. Clamp together until dry.

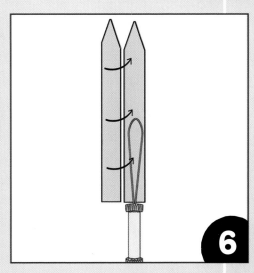

Laying Siege to the Castle

Attackers surrounded a castle prior to beginning an attack, giving those inside time to surrender. When no agreement could be reached, an enemy would begin to lay siege to the castle. This was not an easy matter. Castles were designed to withstand all sorts of attempted break-ins, such as when attackers chipped away at their walls, inserted flaming sticks in the grooves, or launched missiles from catapults that rattled entire foundations.

Another type of catapult, called a mangonel, used twisted ropes to help launch its missile from the end of a beam into fragile wooden roofs. Metal bolts or large stones were repeatedly fired from the ballista, an instrument invented by the Greeks even before Roman times. At the same time, other attackers might attempt to enter the castle from underground. While this was often more difficult, fires could be started at specific points to crack the castle's stone walls.

Through all of this, attackers were often killed or at least injured and

Defending the castle from invaders was the job of the lord's knights. In this fourteenth-century manuscript illumination, knights drop rocks onto the heads of adversaries as one man is trampled in the siege.

weakened by a hail of arrows, stones, and filth that was hurled down upon them during the siege. Because of this, they often formed a "tortoise," by marching with their shields held above their heads for protection.

Battering rams, with a variety of metal pins, were like huge shields on wheels that enemies pushed into castle doorways to bust them down. A trebuchet, a large wooden slingshot on wheels, was often used to swing large rocks toward castle walls or through the wooden roofs of towers. On rarer occasions, enemies put decapitated heads of war victims or diseased animal carcasses in these wooden slingshots. They flung them over castle walls and into courtyards to intimidate their victims or even spread disease. Such extreme tactics were often effective, and there are many records of lords surrendering after only a few days of this treatment.

When gunpowder was available in western Europe, the need for castles decreased. With the invention of artillery, cannon fire could take down stone walls more easily. After that, many castles became useful for other purposes, such as to house a military center or as someone's private residence. Still others fell into disrepair and are now stone ruins.

This is a modern model of a medieval trebuchet, a device for slinging rocks toward castle walls to weaken them or injure its defenders.

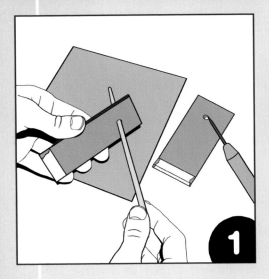

Trebuchet

The trebuchet was among the strongest siege machines available to attackers during medieval times. Create this model of a trebuchet to see how one works.

YOU WILL NEED
- Cardboard
- 2 chopsticks
- Modeling clay
- String
- Matchbox or bottle cap
- Ruler
- Awl/craft knife
- Scissors
- Masking tape
- Burlap
- Glue
- Brown paint and paintbrush

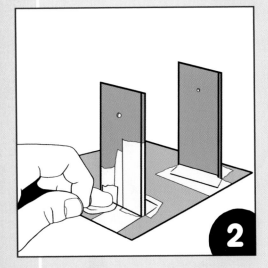

Step 1
Cut a 6-inch square out of cardboard for the trebuchet's base. Cut two 8-inch x ½-inch strips of cardboard for the sides. Fold the two strips in half and tape closed. With an awl, make a hole 1 inch from the top of the fold of each strip. Make the hole large enough to fit a chopstick through it, as shown.

Step 2
Make a fold ½ inch from the bottom of both strips so they stand upright on the base. Tape them to the base about 3 inches apart, as shown.

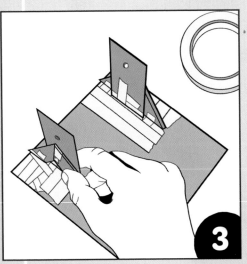

Step 3
Next, cut four strips of cardboard, each 1 x 6 inches. Fold each strip in half so that each length is 3 inches, tape, and make a diagonal cut on the ends of each with scissors. Tape the strips in front of the sides making an upside-down "V" shape. Cover the entire structure with strips of masking tape for further reinforcement.

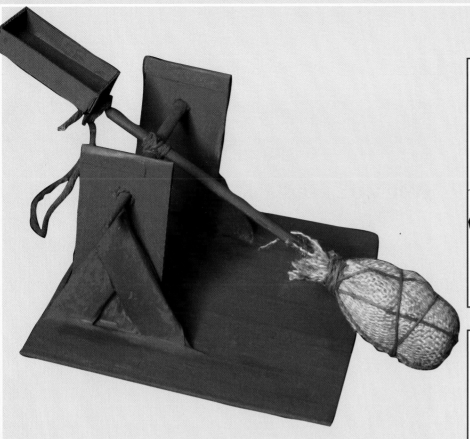

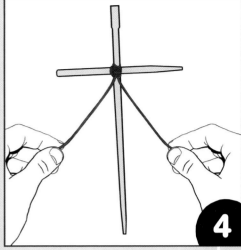

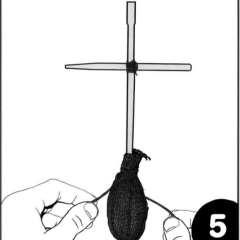

Step 4

Cut one of the chopsticks so that it is about 5 inches long. Bind it to the uncut chopstick with string to make a cross by wrapping it several times with string and then knotting it tightly. Make the cross so the uncut chopstick is vertical with the point on the bottom.

Step 5

Next, roll from modeling clay an oval the size of a small egg and insert the point of the chopstick into it. Cover the clay with a small piece of burlap and secure it in place with string, as shown.

Step 6

Glue the bottom of a matchbox or bottle cap to the end of the chopstick opposite of the clay. Insert the cut chopstick through the holes in the sides of the trebuchet. Tie a string in front of the glued box or cap, as shown.

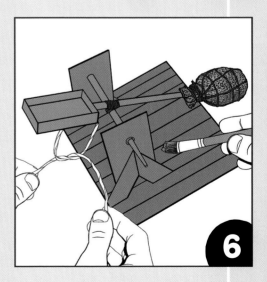

Medieval Dress

The Middle Ages were a very interesting time in terms of male and female fashions and codes of appropriate dress. Medieval hats were worn by all, especially women, since fashion dictated that a woman's hair be completely covered unless she was unmarried. (Medieval women grew their hair long and cared for it with olive oil.) If a married woman was seen walking in public with her hair exposed, she would be judged to have loose morals. Because of this code of social etiquette, women made great use of veils, especially those made from white linen. Hairnets were also worn.

By the twelfth century, most women owned a barbette, a covering that was wrapped across the head, over the ears and under the chin. The wimple was another cloth that was pinned to the sides of a woman's hair or veil and draped down under the chin to cover the throat. It was acceptable, however,

This fifteenth-century illumination shows merchants selling cloth (center), *a pair of nobles* (left), *and a pair of monks* (right). *People of all classes wore hats during the Middle Ages.*

to show a bit of hair from the hairline, or the tips of the ends, as this was considered a modest display of vanity. Noble women took these existing styles and added elaborate headdresses to them. By the thirteenth and fourteenth centuries, women's styles had come to embrace several that were common for men, including the pillbox hat.

Eventually, when it became socially acceptable to see more hair, lengths

were parted in the middle, braided, and then coiled and worn on top of the head. Veils and headpieces were arranged to sit around the coiled braids. Since long hair was a symbol of youthfulness, it became fashionable for a woman's coils to be larger. Soon women began saving their own lengths and even those from other women to increase the size of their coils. By the fifteenth century, styles became even more unique, and fashion styles changed rapidly. Men's tunics got shorter, and the toes of their shoes lengthened.

Clothing was also a way for a woman to show her wealth and vanity. The length of her dress was a good indicator of her wealth and place in society, as was the length and color of a man or woman's overtunic. As people became wealthier, especially by the thirteenth and fourteenth centuries, sumptuary laws were put into effect. These laws outlined who could wear what depending on their social status. Indeed, the traditional aristocrats felt threatened by the "newer rich" who could now afford lavish materials and furs. By restricting what others could wear, they were sure to be set apart from the rest.

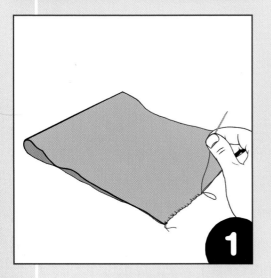

Butterfly Hennin

Cover you hair like medieval women did and try one of the hat styles made famous during the late Middle Ages.

YOU WILL NEED
- Half yard of felt
- Needle and thread
- Ruler
- Scissors
- Wire hanger
- Masking tape
- One yard of transparent fabric

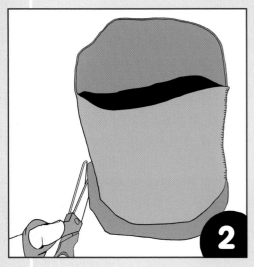

Step 1
Cut a piece of felt that is 7 inches wide and is long enough to wrap around your head completely. Fold the piece in half and sew the ends together making an open cylinder.

Step 2
Next, cut another piece of felt in the shape of a circle that is slightly larger than the circumference of your cylinder, as shown.

Step 3
Sew the circle to the bottom of the cylinder to make the hat.

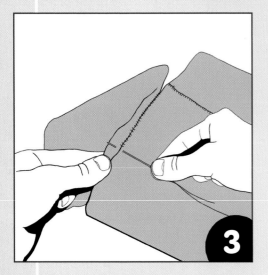

Step 4
With scissors, make two marks in a standard wire hanger about 3 inches from its hook on both sides, as shown. Bend the wire back and forth where you made the marks on the hanger until it breaks in both places. Dispose of the hook. Bend the remaining hanger portion so that you are left with two equal but connected halves. Bend the cut ends upward, as shown. Wrap masking tape around the sharp ends.

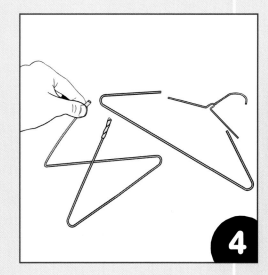

Step 5

Position a 3-inch felt triangle onto the top of your hat in its center. Sew its two sides to the hat leaving the top edge open, as shown. Slip one end of the wire into the pocket, as shown.

Step 6

Fold your transparent fabric in half. Pin it in the center of one edge to the front of the hennin and drape the excess over the wires on both sides, allowing it to flow down to your shoulders. You can also pin it in the back for added stability.

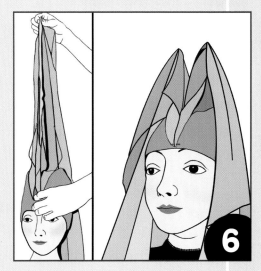

Food and Feasts

A duke and his court are seen dining in the great hall of a fourteenth-century castle. Dining for nobility was a formal affair, with specific attention placed on seating arrangements.

Feasting, as well as famine, was common during the Middle Ages. Medieval feasts, or banquets, were an occasion for celebrating and a show of a king's or lord's wealth and generosity. Specific rules were observed, as some of the lower classes were allowed to eat in the castle's great hall, but only the lord's family and other people of means were served individually. Peasant folks ate their meals seated away from the lord, who was usually positioned in a higher seat to oversee his family and workers. Peasants often ate together in pairs, or in sets of four. They had to share bowls and cups and ate with their hands. In contrast, people of nobility often had their own set of utensils, and their tables were draped in cloth and usually outfitted with candlesticks and saltcellars, which were elaborate glass or silver dishes used to hold the precious commodity. (The expression "above the salt," meaning a person of means, comes from the Middle Ages since only nobles had access to the salt. Peasants sat "below the salt.") Manners were considered important for everyone. Just like today, elbows on the table and talking with one's mouth full of food were considered rude.

Feasts and festivals were elaborate affairs that often lasted several days and employed hundreds of people to do the cooking and preparation. These celebrations usually marked Christian holidays like Christmas and Easter, saints' days, or times special to farming, like the coming harvest. Nobles held feasts for weddings, knights' ceremonies, funerals, or for the completion of an important building. These celebrations called for entertainers of all sorts who

A lord and his lady are entertained by a harp player during a banquet. Also depicted in this manuscript page is a saltcellar—often placed within reach of the highest nobles. Seating at any banquet was based on wealth and class, and the placement of the saltcellar indicated where people should be seated.

performed after the meal was eaten. Musicians, hurdy-gurdy players, minstrels, jugglers, acrobats, and trained animals could often be found inside the castle during these evenings.

A great variety of foods were usually on hand for these events, including beef, pork, mutton, venison, and poultry. Nobles would often try to impress their guests by having the cook stuff smaller animals into larger ones. For example, a quail might be stuffed into a chicken. Or, they might order their cook to sew two types of animals together to make a fantasy animal or put the feathers back on a roasted chicken, then attach it to a duck. Fish was available in abundance, as were foods more commonly eaten by the poor, like eggs, cheese, and vegetables. Wine and ale were served, though wine was enjoyed only by the upper classes. Desserts like tarts, small cakes, and puddings were also served along with candied spices to aid in a celebrant's digestion.

This medieval French saltcellar is made of gold and encrusted with emeralds and pearls. It is part of the collection of the Metropolitan Museum of Art in New York City.

Saltcellar

Give your table medieval distinction by making a replica of this unique saltcellar.

YOU WILL NEED
- Cardboard scraps
- Paper towel roll
- Quart-sized milk carton
- Markers/pencil
- Scissors
- Glue
- Masking tape
- Gold craft paint/brush
- Assorted beads
- Fabric pieces/ribbon
- Bowl/glue-water mixture (for papier-mâché)

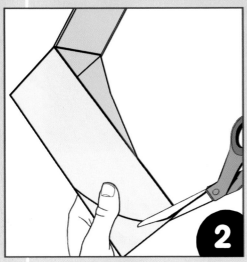

Step 1
Cut the top off of a quart-sized milk carton and discard it. Next, cut along the seams of one side of the carton, as shown. Be sure to keep the cut side attached to the carton's bottom.

Step 2
Lift the cut side of the carton away from you. Fold the remaining three sides into the letter W, as shown. Next, draw a crescent shape on one side of the folded W and cut along those lines, as shown.

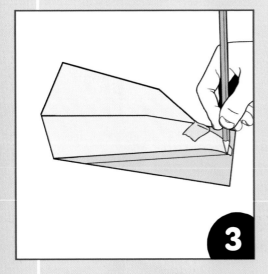

Step 3
Tape the tip of the crescent together and flip the flat, cut side of the carton so that it's on the bottom. Trace around the crescent shape on the remaining flat side, leaving a triangle shape. Cut along traced lines.

Step 4
Slice the paper towel roll lengthwise down the center. Tighten it into a smaller rod and use masking tape to seal it closed in several places. Next, cut a series of slits into one end and fold those out to make several tabs. Attach the roll to the triangle shape by taping the tabs

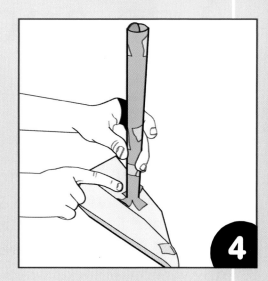

down. Next, use a generous amount of tape to create a flat surface for the bottom of the crescent. Gently curl the point of the triangle away from the rest of the carton with a pencil.

Step 5

Cut an 8-inch circle out of cardboard. Next, slice it to the center of the circle to create a cone. Cut a small X in the center to create four triangular tabs, as shown. Attach the cone to the base of the paper towel roll, creating a bottom for the saltcellar. Papier-mâché the entire saltcellar by dipping strips of paper into your glue/water mixture and applying them to the surface of the saltcellar. Use a brush to remove excess glue. Allow time to dry.

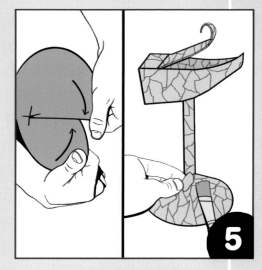

Step 6

Cut a band of cardboard 2 inches in width that winds around the saltcellar's stem. Fold it in half lengthwise. Cut a series of ½-inch slits into it and fan them out before you glue it to the center of the stem. Decorate the saltcellar with decorative trim and beads by gluing them as you wish. Allow for more drying time before painting the entire surface with gold craft paint.

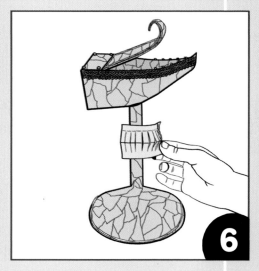

Arts and Leisure

People in the Middle Ages found time for recreation, games, and other leisure activities. Outdoor sports like hunting and hawking and an early version of hockey were hugely popular, as were tournaments. Long winter evenings lent themselves to a variety of indoor pastimes as well. Adults played games we now commonly associate with children such as blind man's bluff, or "hoodman blind," when a person's head was covered by a hood and he or she had to chase other players around the room until another was caught.

Table games like backgammon, draughts (checkers), and fox and geese were enjoyed by most people, especially nobility. Chess was played in the castle regularly, and men were especially delighted by dice games and regularly gambled on their outcome, which was considered a sin.

People of all ages enjoyed listening to musicians, poets, and storytellers. Puppet shows were also a regular form of entertainment for children and adults. Children had few traditional

Several nobles play blind man's bluff in this manuscript illumination. Outdoor games such as this one were as favored during the Middle Ages as they are today.

toys, though boys played mock war games with small-sized helmets and swords. Girls were usually taught how to sew as a pastime. Both girls and boys flew kites and played with marbles, tops, and small models like miniature windmills, rocking chairs, balls, and hoops.

Playing cards made their first European appearance in 1370, though like books, they were something that only nobility could afford. (By far, reading was still considered the most elite form of entertainment since books were so rare.) By the fourteenth century, playing cards were in such demand that they

Hunting was a celebrated social activity of the nobility during the Middle Ages, as was falconry. The hunting party in this image includes men and women as well as dogs, which were used to assist the hunters in finding prey.

were mass-produced. Entire guilds were devoted to their production beginning in the 1420s, especially in Germany. Playing cards were so popular in western Europe that within a decade of their invention laws were made to limit their use, since, like dice games, they were believed to promote the sinful act of gambling.

This set of playing cards is among the world's only complete sets from the medieval period. Card games were popular with all of society and especially with those who enjoyed gambling. Some card games were even outlawed.

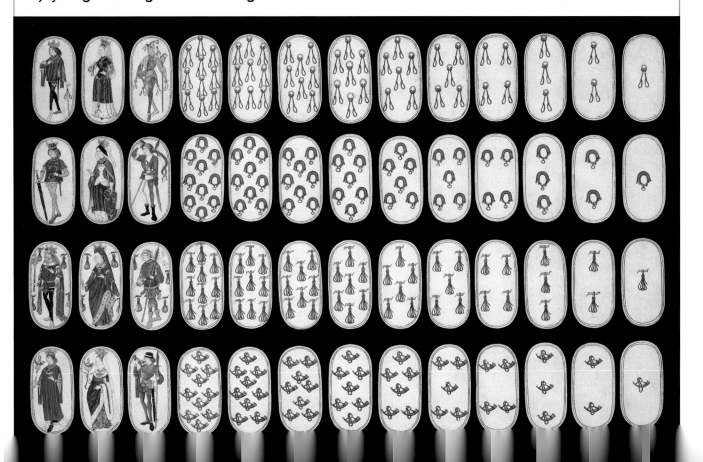

Playing Cards

Make your very own set of playing cards based on a fifteenth-century set from the Netherlands that is housed in the Metropolitan Museum of Art in New York.

YOU WILL NEED
- Cardboard
- String (various widths)
- Scissors
- 4 discarded thread spools
- Toothpicks
- Fine-lined markers
- Craft paint/paintbrushes
- Pencil
- Glue
- Oak tag or white poster board

Step 1
Cut four pieces of cardboard, each 7 inches long and 4 inches wide. These will be your stamps. Using scissors, round off the corners of each stamp. Draw a king, a queen, and a page in pencil on three of the stamps by using simple shapes and connecting lines. Leave the fourth card blank. Trace four 1½-inch circles on cardboard and cut them out. These will be your suit stamps. Draw a symbol on each circle to represent each suit. Medieval cards featured suits with symbols like swords, cups, rings, and batons, but you can also draw hearts, clubs, spades, and diamonds.

Step 2
Glue short, manageable lengths of string to your four stamp designs. The intricacy of your design should dictate the width of your string. Use a toothpick to help guide the string. (For small details like the suit symbols, use a finer string.) Glue a long piece of string around the edge of the four large stamps. After all of the stamp designs have been outlined in glued string (including the circle suits) allow them to dry. Glue each circle suit to a discarded thread spool for printing.

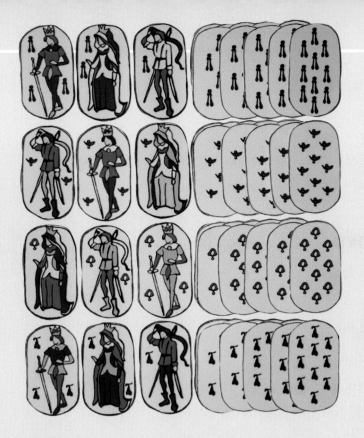

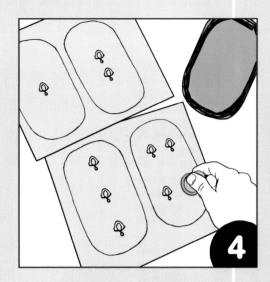

Step 3
With a large brush, coat the stamps with black paint (thinned with water if necessary) as needed for readable prints. Gently set the painted string onto the oak tag or poster board to print the image and then use the palm of your hand to press the designs. Print four of each of the king, queen, and page cards.

Step 4
Take the blank stamp with just the string border and print forty of them. Next, print a suit design within the printed border of each to make up the ten cards in each suit. Repeat this step until you have completed all four suits, or forty cards.

Step 5
Use the suit stamps to add a symbol to each of the king, queen, and page cards.

Step 6
Color your cards with paints or markers as you desire. When finished, cut the cards out with scissors and play a game with a friend!

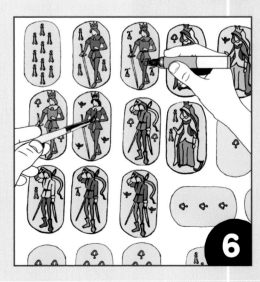

TIMELINE

A.D. **313**   Constantine imposes the Edict of Milan, preaching tolerance for Christianity.

410   Visigoths sack Rome.

circa 476   The Roman Empire falls.

476–1000   The period historians sometimes refer to as Europe's Dark Ages.

circa 700   Feudal system is established in France.

711   Muslims invade Spain.

768   Charlemagne becomes king of the Franks.

793   Beginning of Viking raids in England.

1066   William the Conqueror conquers England.

1095   Pope Urban II urges Christian knights to defend Christianity.

1096–1291   The Christian Crusades are launched to recapture the Holy Land from Muslims.

1161   First guilds are established; the era of cathedral-building begins.

1171   The Bank of Venice opens.

1179   The third Lateran Council decrees all cathedrals must have schools.

1180   Windmills first appear in Europe.

1215   The fourth Lateran Council requires Jews to wear identifying badges; signing of the Magna Carta.

1241   Mongols invade Europe.

1271   Marco Polo travels to Asia.

1300   Feudalism ends.

1314–1322   The great famine (alternate droughts and heavy rains in northern Europe).

1337–1453   Hundred Years' War between England and France.

1347–1530   The plague kills about 25 million people throughout Europe.

1381   Peasants' Revolt.

1453   The fall of Constantinople to Ottoman Turks (often taken as end of Middle Ages).

GLOSSARY

bailiff A castle servant who took care of the castle property.

barbican A stone structure built on the outside of a castle that housed the outer door or entrance gate.

Bayeux Tapestry Embroidery commissioned in the 1070s that tells the story of the Norman conquest.

chain mail Flexible armor made of interlinked metal rings.

chapel Smaller rooms for worship within a castle or cathedral.

concentric castle A castle designed with one or more rings of defensive walls.

crenellation The serrated or toothed upper battlement of a castle wall that helped protect knights while they shot arrows at invaders.

Crusades Religious wars fought between Christians and Muslims during the Middle Ages.

curtain A stone wall around a castle, usually with towers.

donjon The Norman name for a castle keep, from which the English word "dungeon" is derived.

garrison The group of knights who protected the castle.

great hall The large, main room inside a castle.

hurdy-gurdy A stringed instrument that is sounded by a rotating wheel.

keep The large central fortress in a castle.

lord A male knight and/or noble who was given a fief (plot of land) by the king.

machicolation Openings in the floor of an overhanging structure, designed to allow the defenders to drop hot oil onto attackers.

mangonel A type of medieval catapult that used twisting ropes to hurl rocks toward castle walls.

portcullis A heavy metal door, often grated, that slid down at a castle's entrance in order to provide security.

trebuchet A simple wooden device, like a gigantic slingshot, that was used to hurl boulders into or toward a castle.

turret A small ornamented tower or tower-shaped projection on a castle.

FOR MORE INFORMATION

Columbia University Medieval Guild
602 Philosophy Hall
Columbia University
New York, NY 10027
Web site: http://www.cc.columbia.edu/
    cu/medieval

The Metropolitan Museum of Art
1000 Fifth Avenue
New York, NY 10028-0198
(212) 535-7710
Web site: http://www.metmuseum.org

WEB SITES

Due to the changing nature of Internet links, the Rosen Publishing Group, Inc., has developed an online list of Web sites related to the subject of this book. This site is updated regularly. Please use the link below to access the list:

http://www.rosenlinks.com/ccma/mcas

FOR FURTHER READING

Bergin, Mark. *Castle*. London, England: Hodder Wayland, 2001.

Gravett, Christopher. *Castle (Eyewitness Guides)*. London, England: Dorling Kindersley, Ltd., 2004.

Hilliam, David. *Castles and Cathedrals: The Great Buildings of Medieval Times* (The Library of the Middle Ages). New York, NY: The Rosen Publishing Group, 2004.

Newman, Paul B. *Daily Life in the Middle Ages*. Jefferson, NC: McFarland & Company, 2004.

Taylor, Barbara. *World of Castles*. Bath, England: Southwater, 2000.

INDEX

ABOUT THE AUTHOR/ILLUSTRATOR

Joann Jovinelly and Jason Netelkos have collaborated on many educational projects for young people. This is their second crafts series encouraging youngsters to learn history through hands-on projects. Their first series, Crafts of the Ancient World, was published by the Rosen Publishing Group in 2001. They live in New York City.

PHOTO CREDITS

Cover (center), p. 37 (bottom) Metropolitan Museum of Art, The Cloisters Collection, 1983 (1983.434); pp. 4, 13 (top) Réunion des Musées Nationaux/Art Resource, NY; p. 5 Bildarchiv Preussischer Kulturbesitz/Art Resource, NY; p. 7 © Robert Estall photo agency/Alamy; p. 9 © F. Damm/zefa/Corbis; p. 10 HIP/Art Resource, NY; pp. 12, 21 (top), Erich Lessing/Art Resource, NY; p. 13 (bottom) © Derek Croucher/Corbis; pp. 16, 17 (top) Bibliothèque nationale de France; p. 17 (bottom) © Francis G. Mayer/Corbis; pp. 20, 25 (bottom) Giraudon/Art Resource, NY; p. 21 (bottom) Bibliotheque de L'Arsenal, Paris, France, Index/Bridgeman Art Library p. 24 © Archivo Iconografico, S.A./Corbis; p. 25 (top) The Art Archive/ Biblioteca Comunale Palermo/Dagli Orti; p. 28 The Art Archive/University Library Heidelerg/Dagli Orti; p. 29 (top) SEF/Art Resource, NY; p. 29 (bottom) Geoff Dann © Dorling Kindersley; p. 32 The Art Archive/Bibliothéque Municipale Rouen/ Dagli Orti; p. 33 (top) The Art Archive/Biblioteca Capitolare Verona/Dagli Orti; p. 33 (bottom) © Historical Picture Archive/Corbis; p. 36 Snark/Art Resource, NY; p. 37 (top) The Art Archive/Bodleian Library Oxford; p. 40 British Library, London, UK/Bridgeman Art Library; p. 41 (top) Scala/Art Resource, NY; p. 41 (bottom) Metropolitan Museum of Art, The Cloisters Collection, 1983 (1983.515.1-.52). All crafts designed by Jason Netelkos and Joann Jovinelly. All craft illustrations by Jason Netelkos. All craft photography by Joann Jovinelly.

Special thanks to Christina Burfield for her continued support and encouragement.

Designer: Evelyn Horovicz; Editor: Leigh Ann Cobb
Photo Researcher: Nicole DiMella